Mother Jones

One Woman's Fight for Labor

Mother Jones

One Woman's Fight for Labor

BETSY HARVEY KRAFT

Clarion Books/New York

Frontispiece: *Mother Jones helps a miner's daughter put on her new shoes.*

Clarion Books
a Houghton Mifflin Company imprint
215 Park Avenue South, New York, NY 10003
Text copyright © 1995 by Betsy Harvey Kraft

Type is 13/16 Sabon
Book design by Carol Goldenberg
All rights reserved.
For information about permission to reproduce selections from
this book, write to Permissions, Houghton Mifflin Company,
215 Park Avenue South, New York, NY 10003.
Printed in the USA.

Library of Congress Cataloging-in-Publication Data
Kraft, Betsy Harvey.
     Mother Jones : one woman's fight for labor / by Betsy Harvey
Kraft.
          p.   cm.
     Includes bibliographical references and index.
     ISBN 0-395-67163-9
     1. Jones, Mother, 1843?–1930—Juvenile literature.   2.
Women labor leaders—United States—Biography—Juvenile
literature.   3. Trade unions—Coal miners—Organizing—United
States—History—Juvenile literature.   [1. Jones, Mother,
1843?–1930.   2. Labor leaders.   3. Women—Biography.]   I.
Title.
HD8073.J6K73   1995
331.88'092—dc20
[B]   94-19715
                                                        CIP
                                                         AC

HOR 10   9   8   7   6   5   4   3   2   1

To Women of Courage Everywhere

Contents

Mother Jones

One Woman's Fight for Labor

CHAPTER ONE

"I Have Been in Jail More than Once"

THE WOMAN ON THE STEPS of the state capitol was a tiny thing. She wore a black dress with a lace collar and steel-rimmed glasses. Her snowy hair, pulled in a tight knot, was topped by a black straw hat decorated with lavender ribbons. She was almost eighty years old and stood five feet tall. From her looks, she might have been someone's frail grandmother surrounded by a sea of rowdy West Virginia coal miners.

Then she began to speak. Her voice, low and forceful, carrying a trace of her Irish heritage, rang out through the gathered crowd.

"I have been in jail more than once, and I expect to go again. If you are too cowardly to fight, I will fight.

"Now my boys, you are mine. We have fought together, we have marched together, but I can see victory in the heavens for you. I can see the hand above you guiding and inspiring you to move onward and upward. . . . We must redeem the world."

The gathered miners and their families listened spellbound. She urged the men to action and appealed to their sense of justice and self-respect. She lambasted their bosses and ridiculed their politicians. You have power, she told her listeners, power to change the world. She spoke for an hour and a half, and when she concluded the members of the audience cheered till they were hoarse.

This was Mother Jones, one of America's most effective union organizers. At a time in United States history when only a handful of women were active in politics or spoke out in public, Mother Jones was a fearless crusader for the rights of American laborers. She took on wealthy business tycoons and became a nationally known champion for children who labored in the textile mills.

She publicly disclosed the unsavory working conditions for women employed in the brewing industry and used her flamboyant speaking style to mobilize steel workers seeking higher wages.

She used congressional hearings to bully senators and congressmen and was fearless in the face of presidents and the country's richest industrialists. She took on the cause of the Mexican revolutionaries who she felt were being treated unjustly by their own government and raised money for their defense. Late in life she even spoke out against the men who led the unions she had helped to form. Their greed and excess, she felt, were jeopardizing the gains she and others had fought for so long and hard.

Most of all, Mother Jones was known as the "miners' angel." She was a tireless supporter of the men and women in coal camps from West Virginia to Colorado, and she literally put her life on the line to support the miners in the often bloody struggle for safer working conditions and better pay.

She also went to jail for them. In 1913, when the miners of West Virginia were fighting for the right to organize unions, Mother Jones was arrested, illegally she claimed, for giving speeches in support of their cause. She spent three months in jail and gained so much national attention for the cause of the miners that the governor was relieved to let her go.

Mother Jones had a special attachment to the people of the coal fields. She referred to the miners as "her boys" and it was with them she earned the name of "Mother." As a woman and an outsider, she fearlessly challenged the gun-toting guards and the mine owners, and the miners loved her for it. In her autobiography she tells a story about coming to Virginia:

"There was a strike in the Dietz mines and the boys had sent for me.

When I got off the train at Norton a fellow walked up to me and asked me if I were Mother Jones.

" 'Yes, I am Mother Jones.'

"He looked terribly frightened. 'The superintendent told me that if you came down here he would blow out your brains. He said he didn't want to see you 'round these parts.'

" 'You tell the superintendent that I am not coming to see him anyway. I am coming to see the miners.' "

It was this feistiness and boldness that inspired the miners and made Mother Jones their champion. But not everyone shared their enthusiasm for the fiery, Irish-born organizer.

In Colorado, where she led striking coal miners, the head of the state's militia called her "dangerous because she inflames the minds of the strikers." He also criticized her speeches, which he said were crude and full of profanity. The state's governor, Elias Ammons, flatly declared, "She has no business here."

She was equally unpopular among the mine owners and many of the state officials in West Virginia. They distributed pamphlets that portrayed her as an atheist and a cold-blooded advocate of violence and brutality. She was irreverent and critical of the church, they said. And, in a blow to her saintly image, they accused her of once having earned her living as a prostitute.

With any historic figure, it is often hard to separate fact from fiction. Much of the labor movement in America took place on unruly picket lines or in the tent camps of Appalachia and the West where scholarship and careful record-keeping were nonexistent. Feelings on both sides of the labor issue ran high and both sides exaggerated their own virtues and the other's evils. Mother Jones was no exception. Her autobiography is full of vain references to her own importance, and her own portrayal of her role in the labor movement does not always coincide with other accounts. Occasionally she deliberately misrepresented the facts to gain support for what she thought was right.

But she believed deeply in her cause and she knew her gift of oratory could mobilize workers to help change the face of a nation. And she was proud of her power. When a college professor once introduced her to an audience as a "great humanitarian" she snapped, "Get it right. I'm not a humanitarian. I'm a hell-raiser."

A look at her life indicates that she and the professor were both right. She *was* a humanitarian and she was a hell-raiser. To follow her transformation from a young seamstress and schoolteacher to a labor agitator is to follow the history of the United States through some of its most volatile times.

CHAPTER TWO

"My People Were Poor"

MOTHER JONES IS KNOWN for her work in America, but throughout her long life she remained as Irish as St. Patrick's Day. She was born Mary Harris in the city of Cork, Ireland, probably in the late 1830s. Her family was Catholic and to be Catholic in Cork meant that she learned early on about discrimination and oppression.

The English, who ruled the country to their north, insisted that everyone in Ireland belong to the protestant Church of England. Catholics were scorned and denied the rights granted to others living in Ireland. England did everything it could to make Catholics second-class citizens: they were not allowed to vote, they could not hold office, they could not attend mass, and they could not buy land.

Fired by the success of the American colonies, the Irish too hoped to shake off England's domination. But the British soldiers brutally put down the uprisings of the Irish rebels. One of Mary's early childhood memories was seeing British soldiers march through the streets carrying the severed heads of Irish rebels on pikes. Torture was common. Those who dared to challenge British rule were often flogged until they begged to be shot.

Violence was one part of Mary's early life. Poverty was another. "My people were poor," Mother Jones wrote years later in her autobiography. "For generations they had fought for Ireland's freedom. . . . Many of my folks have died in that struggle."

An artist shows cotters, living in Ireland around the time of Mary's birth, being evicted from their homes by an unsympathetic landlord.

Details of her early years are murky, but probably her father was a cotter, a peasant who lived on the land and made his living as the farmer of a small plot of land owned by a wealthy landlord. The peasants were called cotters because they lived in cottages. The landlords raised their rent often and evicted the cotters if they could not keep up with their payments.

Famine was also common during this period in Ireland. Potatoes were the mainstay of the Irish diet, but in the 1830s and '40s even the potatoes disappeared. During those years a blight devastated Ireland's potato crop and thousands of peasants thronged the roads and city streets, starving and desperate for food.

Since Mary's family was both Catholic and poor, she knew double oppression. But her family, like many of their Cork neighbors, did not accept their oppression. Instead, they fought back. Throughout Ireland there were rebels, both Catholic and Protestant, who protested unfair rule by England.

One eloquent Catholic dissenter was Daniel O'Connell, who used his gift of oratory to inspire fellow dissenters to rise up against the British. He combined his Irish charm with persuasive oratory. One farmer who heard him speak said O'Connell's was a voice "you'd hear a mile off as if it were coming through honey." If Mary did not actually hear him, she probably knew of him, and some part of her young girl's mind may have absorbed the idea that the spoken word could be a powerful tool in fighting injustice.

Mary's family was more direct in its dissent. They fought violence with violence. Her grandfather was hanged as a traitor to the crown because he fought against British rule, and her father was a Cork rebel, perhaps one of the men who rode through the country at night burning the barns of English landlords. When she was just a young girl, British soldiers ransacked the Harris cottage, even tearing down the chimney in their search for Mary's father.

Forced to leave Ireland for defying the English, Richard Harris fled the country and headed for the United States and later Canada. The rest of the family later sailed to join him, probably in the early 1840s when Mary was still very young. The ship Mary and her family sailed on most likely carried far too many passengers for its size and the emigrants probably slept exposed to the elements on deck. Food was as scarce as or scarcer than it had been in Ireland.

It must have been a dramatic moment when the family was reunited. Together again, they had the opportunity for a new start. Their new life would not be easy, but the horrors of Irish repression and hunger no longer cast their terrifying shadows over the Harrises' lives.

Richard Harris found work on the canals in upstate New York, along with many other newly arrived immigrants from Ireland. When work on that project was over, he moved to Toronto, where he began work on the Canadian railroads. Mary grew up there, attending public schools and excelling in debate. After her secondary schooling, she trained to become a teacher. "Dressmaking too I learned proficiently," she wrote in her autobiography.

Though she was born in Ireland and brought up in Canada, Mother Jones always emphasized that she was an American citizen. "Of that citizenship I have ever been proud," she wrote. Certainly she considered herself thoroughly American and she did most of her important work in the United States. But until she died, she spoke with a charming Irish brogue.

Like many other Irish, she was a fighter for the poor and oppressed. She had the gift of oratory, was fearless in facing down opposition, knew the rigors of poverty, and was undaunted by living in what others considered harsh and dangerous conditions. Surely her early years in Ireland had something to do with guiding her toward the path she chose to walk in later life.

At the time of her death, a newspaper quoted a friend as saying, "If Mother Jones had stayed in Ireland, she probably would have been hanged . . . or else, she would have been President of the Irish Republic."

She chose a different path, but one that was scarcely less dramatic.

CHAPTER THREE

"I Sat Alone Through Nights of Grief"

For young immigrant women like Mary, two professions were considered respectable, dressmaking and teaching school. Mary was trained in both. Her first job took her from Canada to New England, where she worked briefly as a tutor before she moved on to Monroe, Michigan, to teach in a Catholic convent school for girls. Her salary there was $36.40 for the year.

Mary found that she preferred dressmaking to "bossing little children," and around 1860 she moved to Chicago, where there was a demand for young women trained as seamstresses. But Mary seldom stayed in one place for long and soon she had left that city to move south to Memphis, Tennessee, where she was back to "bossing" as a teacher.

In Memphis, Mary met and married George Jones. They set up housekeeping in 1861 in the section of town where the working poor lived. George worked in a foundry and was an enthusiastic member of the Iron Molders Union, one of the country's earliest organized trade groups.

Mary probably had little inkling then that unions such as the one George belonged to would become the central force in her future. Her life was focused on her role as a wife and mother of four young children at the time when the bloody, divisive Civil War was raging in the rest of the country. Although Memphis was important in the Civil War, it was spared the devastation suffered by many other southern cities. But in 1862, Yankee forces invaded Memphis and claimed it for the north.

With the end of the Civil War, residents of Memphis must have felt a tremendous sense of relief. But the city soon suffered another tragedy, a series of epidemics of yellow fever. The disease, for which there was then neither a vaccine nor a cure, occurred mostly in warm, humid regions. The virus was carried by mosquitoes which found homes in the open sewers and standing water common in the poorer sections of town. Mary and her family lived in such an area.

In 1867, terrified residents of the community began to recognize the symptoms of the deadly disease—fever, chills, painful joints, vomiting, convulsions, and coma. When the summer was over, two hundred were dead. Among them were Mary's four young children and her husband.

"The rich and the well-to-do fled the city," Mary wrote bitterly years later in her autobiography. "The poor could not afford nurses. Across the street from me, ten persons lay dead from the plague. The dead surrounded us. They were buried at night, quickly and without ceremony. All about my house I could hear weeping and the cries of delirium. One by one, my four little children sickened and died. I washed their little bodies and got them ready for burial. My husband caught the fever and died. I sat alone through nights of grief. No one came to me. No one could. Other homes were as stricken as was mine. All day long, all night long, I heard the grating of the wheels of the death cart."

Mary seldom spoke of her family after the staggering loss she suffered in Memphis. During her childhood in Ireland she had known famine and violence, but nothing could have prepared her for this kind of personal pain. Perhaps her silence on the subject tells us that the loss was too great to think about. As a matter of emotional survival perhaps she had to turn her thoughts to other matters.

Soon she had submerged her own personal grief and began helping others. "After the union had buried my husband, I got a permit to nurse the sufferers. This I did until the plague was stamped out."

Mary had lived in Memphis for more than six years, but it could not have seemed like home without her children and husband. Once again she uprooted herself and returned to Chicago, where she again took up dressmaking. This time she opened a shop with another woman, in a small space on Washington Street in the city's center.

Chicago, like Ireland, was to play a key role in Mary's life. In the early 1830s it was little more than a midwestern settlement on Lake Michigan with forty houses and two hundred inhabitants. By 1860, when the Republican convention met there to nominate Abraham Lincoln to run for president of the United States, it was the largest city in the Midwest. By the end of the Civil War its population had grown to

An immigrant mother and her children in a Chicago tenement.

300,000. It was now a major railroad hub with almost one hundred trains arriving and departing each day.

When Mary arrived there for the second time in 1867, it was a new home to tens of thousands of immigrants who had poured in from Germany, Ireland, Italy, Greece, and other countries. They came to Chicago for one reason—jobs. Here they could hope to find work with the railroads or in the stockyards or the meatpacking houses. Or perhaps they would sign on at the McCormick Reaper Works south of the city where they would help manufacture the giant machines that cut the grain in the fertile fields of the Midwest.

These newly arrived immigrants lived in crowded, dark tenements, with several families often sharing one room in order to pay the high rents charged by their landlords. Pay was low and hours were long. Grown men trying to support a family often worked sixteen hours a day for as little as two dollars. One salary was seldom enough to support an immigrant family, so women and children joined the workforce.

Jane Addams, who founded an immigrant settlement house in Chicago (and was later a friend of Mother Jones) told of children who worked in a candy factory from 7 A.M. to 9 P.M. each day during the Christmas season. They were allowed twenty minutes for lunch, had no supper, and earned less than seventy-five cents a day.

As brutal as this way of life may have been, it was worse to have no job at all. And in the 1870s many of Chicago's immigrants, like others across the nation, found themselves out of work. Wealthy bankers had invested heavily in government certificates and lost millions when the price of gold fell dramatically. The owners of factories, mines, and railroads held on to what money they could by reducing the wages of many of their workers and firing others. It was the beginning of more than twenty years of on-and-off depressions and hard times for the working poor.

In her shop on Washington Street, Mary sewed elaborate gowns for Chicago's wealthy matrons. From her window there she could see ragtag children and unemployed workmen passing by, huddled against the icy winds blowing off Lake Michigan.

Immigrant women working in New York's garment industry. Drawing from
Frank Leslie's Illustrated Newspaper.

Unemployed men in Chicago during the late 1800s. Drawing from Harper's Weekly.

"We worked for the aristocrats of Chicago, and I had ample opportunity to observe the luxury and extravagance of their lives. Often while sewing for the lords and barons who lived in magnificent houses on Lake Shore Drive we would look out of the plate glass windows and see the poor, shivering wretches, jobless and hungry, walking along the frozen lake front. The contrast of their condition with that of the tropical comfort of the people for whom I sewed was painful to me. My employers seemed neither to notice nor to care."

Despite the financial plight of other immigrants, Mary was able to make a living. It would seem that her life had finally settled into some kind of order and calm after her traumatic and tragic early years, and dressmaking provided her with a steady, if not large, income. But life was not destined to be calm or orderly for Mary. Another tragedy was to transform her life once again—the Great Chicago Fire.

It began the evening of October 8, 1871, when a fire broke out on the city's west side, where immigrants crowded into a labyrinth of streets lined with small houses. The summer had been a dry one and in a city

The Chicago fire of 1871 left Mother Jones homeless and jobless. Print by Currier & Ives.

where offices, stores, houses, and even some of the streets were constructed from wood, fire was a continual threat.

The city's firemen were already exhausted from having fought two earlier fires and within minutes the new one became a major blaze. It consumed several city blocks before the wind shifted toward the east, sweeping the fire toward the center of the city. It roared through heavily populated areas and reached the commercial section, leaving a trail of devastation in its wake. When rain finally tamed the fire after two days of wild burning, three hundred people were dead and 100,000 were without homes. Virtually all the shops, offices, factories, boarding-houses, homes, and hotels in the area were blackened chars.

Mary's shop, her home, and her livelihood were among the ruins, leaving her to start over, once again.

CHAPTER FOUR

"A Quick Brain and an Even Quicker Tongue"

THE GREAT FIRE OF 1871 changed Chicago and it changed Mary Jones. The few buildings that remained standing after the fire soon became havens for people left without homes. Old St. Mary's Church, around the corner from her devastated shop, offered shelter for Mary and others who had been burned out. She slept and ate there until she was able to find a new place to live.

In the evenings following the fire, Mary discovered the headquarters of the Knights of Labor and began to spend time there. "The Knights of Labor was the labor organization of those days," she wrote in her autobiography. "I used to spend my evenings at their meetings, listening to splendid speakers." What she learned at these lectures changed her from a quiet, unknown seamstress into a radical union organizer.

Immigrants were pouring into Chicago by the thousands looking for work. The city had rebuilt itself with amazing speed after the fire. The Second City, as it was now called, needed laborers to work in its growing industries. Immigrants took these low-paying, often dangerous jobs.

Throughout the country, workers were beginning to join together into groups in hopes of bettering their working conditions. In 1860

Terrance Powderly at a Knights of Labor convention in 1886. Drawing from Frank Leslie's Illustrated Newspaper.

employees of the shoe manufacturers had gone on strike in Lynn, Massachusetts, demanding higher pay and better working conditions. By the 1870s, there were about thirty national unions. Most of them were for skilled laborers who worked in one particular trade or craft. The Knights of Labor, founded in 1869, welcomed all workers into membership, whether they were skilled or unskilled, immigrant or native, black or white, male or female.

One of Mary's favorite lecturers was Terrance Powderly. He and other leaders in the Knights told the immigrant laborers that they should educate themselves, organize, and confront their bosses to demand better conditions.

A certificate honoring Terrance Powderly.

Chicago's working poor flocked to the Knights' meetings. They welcomed the chance to speak without fear about the anger they felt toward their bosses. Here they could freely discuss ways to gain more power in the workplace. At Knights' halls throughout the country laborers could shop at a cooperative store, hear a lecture, or read a book or newspaper. On Sundays, their one day off, workers might go on a Knights' picnic. On Saturday night, they might live it up a little at one of their dances. The organization provided a sense of hope for their lives.

Mary found the meetings spellbinding. At one of the first lectures she attended she rose to her feet and challenged Powderly with a question. He remembered her in his autobiography as "a young seamstress . . . good looking, with a quick brain and an even quicker tongue." During their discussions of labor issues they formed a fast and lasting friendship.

While Mary was getting her education in labor issues from the Knights of Labor, other unions were forming. Workers all over the United States were discontented with their living conditions and the treatment they received on their jobs. In Pennsylvania a group of Irish coal miners called the Molly Maguires formed a secret society. They terrified the mine owners and managers in an effort to make them recognize the miners' right to belong to a union. The large coal and rail companies were determined to crush the group. They hired a spy to infiltrate the Molly Maguires and in 1875 several members were arrested and tried for murder. During the proceedings it was clear that it was the labor movement that was on trial, not the men accused, and ten of the Molly Maguires were hanged.

In those days several states had laws allowing workers to join unions, but employers made it difficult for them to belong. In the coal mines, for instance, if a miner joined a union, he might be placed in a part of the mine where it was impossible to work. Or the materials he needed would not show up. That meant he could not mine coal and would not receive any wages.

The attempt to organize unions was also hurt by the depression. The

Pennsylvania coal miners draw a coded map on stone showing the location of a secret union meeting. Drawing from Harper's Weekly.

The great rail strike of 1877 began in Martinsburg, West Virginia. Drawing from Frank Leslie's Illustrated Newspaper.

hard financial times that Mary had witnessed in Chicago continued throughout the 1870s and '80s. Men were afraid of losing their jobs and were willing to put up with terrible conditions and low pay. "In the cities there was hunger and rags and despair," Mary recalled later.

Among the groups that suffered the most were the railroad workers. They worked fifteen to eighteen hours a day and lived in hovels next to the railroad tracks. The owners of the railroads made fortunes but their workers often made less than a dollar a day.

Work on the railroads was dangerous. Brakemen had to jump from car to car to set the hand brakes and often they were maimed or killed when they lost their footing and fell between the cars. The firemen who stoked the engine's steam furnace with coal or wood had to crawl over hot boilers and were often badly burned. During the depression years, their wages were cut several times.

The last straw for the rail workers came in July 1877. The Baltimore and Ohio Railroad had followed the lead of other major railroads and

Federal troops and striking railroad workers fight a bloody battle in Maryland during the Great Uprising. Drawing from Frank Leslie's Illustrated Newspaper.

cut the wages of its employees once again—this time by ten percent. The desperate workers decided to take action.

Brakemen and firemen in Martinsburg, West Virginia, refused to work unless the pay cuts were canceled. The company refused and two days later more than one thousand freight cars blocked the rails and prevented trains from getting through. Coal miners from the area joined in the strike. First state, then federal troops were sent in to quiet the riot, but sympathetic workers in other parts of the country took to the streets in support.

In Baltimore eleven strikers were shot and killed by state troops. When strikers in Pittsburgh shut down the trains there, they were joined by workers from nearby mines, mills, and factories. The towns-people of Pittsburgh were no lovers of the railroads, and many joined in the protest on the side of the workers. Even the Pittsburgh militia sided with the strikers.

Then troops called in from Philadelphia arrived and fired on a crowd

Rail workers attack "scabs" who took their jobs during a Chicago strike. Drawing from Frank Leslie's Illustrated Newspaper.

The Pittsburgh train station goes up in flames during the Great Uprising. Drawing from Frank Leslie's Illustrated Newspaper.

of protesters. Twenty people, including a woman and three children, were killed. Strikers retaliated by setting fire to the building where the militia was housed. Finally, federal troops were called in.

By now the strikers were out of control. The strike had spread across the nation, and communities were terrified of the unleashed power of the working class. Trains stood silent in the yards of the Midwest, Texas, and San Francisco. In Chicago, the strike engulfed the city. Shopowners closed down their operations in support of the strike. The city's mayor ordered the police to fire directly into the crowds of strikers, and two men were killed.

The Great Uprising, as it was called, lasted two weeks. When it was over, one hundred people were dead and the cost of damage to businesses ran into millions of dollars. Workers went back to their jobs having won nothing. The wage cuts remained in effect. Conditions had not improved. Many workers were blacklisted: their bosses knew they had been part of the strike and they could not get their old jobs back or work for any other company. Bitterest of all, labor had learned that in a major strike they could not count on government to support or protect them.

Mother Jones, of course, sided with the strikers. She blamed the riots on thugs hired by businesses in an attempt to make the strikers look bad.

"Then and there I learned in the early part of my career that labor must bear the cross for others' sins, must be the vicarious sufferer for the wrongs that others do . . . Hand in hand with the growth of factories . . . came anti-labor legislation. Came strikes. Came violence. Came the belief in the hearts and minds of the workers that legislatures but carry out the will of the industrialists."

The dream of an eight-hour day portrayed in an early labor-movement certificate.

CHAPTER FIVE

Eight Hours a Day

IN SPITE OF SETBACKS, the fighting spirit of America's laborers would not go away. By the early 1880s Mary had joined with the Knights of Labor in its call for an eight-hour workday.

Many industrial workers spent fourteen, sometimes eighteen hours a day at their jobs. The Knights, with Terrance Powderly now their president, had decided to make government their ally rather than their enemy. They began to elect pro-labor candidates to public office. Their demands were simple: no child labor, safe work conditions, and paid medical care for injuries suffered on the job. But most important, they wanted an eight-hour day.

The Knights were not the only group to call for the eight-hour day. Anarchists, a group of radicals who wanted America's business system destroyed and turned over to its laborers, had made the shorter work-day their most fervent cause. Mary lived in Chicago at a time when the anarchists were considered a grave threat by business owners in the United States. The black flag, the symbol of their group, was regarded by many with terror.

Mary remembered meetings the anarchists held on the shores of Lake Michigan. Though she never endorsed their philosophy, she listened to what they had to say. Meanwhile, she recalled, employers were meeting to discuss means of killing the eight-hour movement "which was to be ushered in by a general strike." Employers used fear of the anarchists to turn many Chicago residents against the shorter workday. The city was divided, Mary recalled: the workers, poor and powerless, against their rich and powerful employers.

In her autobiography, Mary recalled a Christmas Day parade of "hundreds of poverty-stricken people in rags and tatters, in thin clothes, in wretched shoes," who paraded on fashionable Prairie Avenue carrying the black flag in front of the mansions of the rich. Mary thought the parade was "an insane move on the part of the anarchists," since it would make the rich, the police, and the public more frightened and less sympathetic to the concerns of the workers.

Terrance Powderly, like Mary, thought the anarchists were too radical. In general he did not support the idea of strikes as a way of gaining reforms. But he strongly supported the eight-hour day, and in the spring of 1886, labor groups from all over the country staged a one-day strike in favor of it.

Thousands of Knights of Labor members joined in the May strike. In Chicago alone, forty thousand laborers refused to work and set up picket lines outside the factories and businesses. Newspapers in Chicago and other cities had predicted violence and encouraged a feeling of fear. The strike went off without event, however, and some employers even agreed to the workers' pleas.

In Chicago, the McCormick Reaper Works refused to meet the workers' demands. The plant managers hired strikebreakers, people who took the strikers' jobs and kept the plants open, giving the strikers less bargaining power. The workers called the strikebreakers "scabs."

Two days after the general strike, regular employees picketed the plant and threw rocks at the scabs. The police were called in to restore order and shot six of the strikers dead and wounded dozens more. Chicago's anarchists called for a demonstration to protest the killings. The location was to be Haymarket Square, located in a rundown section of town west of the city's center.

It rained the night of the Haymarket rally and the crowd was smaller than the anarchists wanted or expected. The newspapers and police

Police firing into the crowd at Haymarket Square. Drawing from Harper's Weekly.

Anarchists convicted in Haymarket Square riot prepare to face the gallows. Drawing from Frank Leslie's Illustrated Newspaper.

had warned the public of possible violence, but everything proceeded peacefully. The mayor even visited the scene and found it calm so he told the police to reduce their numbers. Just after he left, 180 policemen marched into the square and ordered the people to stop the meeting. At that moment an explosion, caused by a bomb, ripped through the crowd and killed seven policemen. The police responded instantly by firing into the crowd. One protester was killed and several injured.

No one ever knew for sure who threw the bomb, but the press, police, and general public immediately blamed the Haymarket Square event on the anarchists. Eight anarchists were arrested, and after a trial of much hysteria and virtually no evidence, four were hanged. One committed suicide and three remained in prison until they were pardoned years later by Illinois governor John Altgeld.

The Haymarket Square incident was a blow to the labor movement in general and the Knights of Labor in particular. The Knights refused to provide any support for the accused men and wrote speeches and articles to separate their organization from the event. Even so, the general public had become suspicious of all labor groups, whether or not they included anarchists. Within two years the membership of the Knights had dropped dramatically. Mary was one of the ones who remained loyal to the organization.

KING DEBS.

A political cartoon illustrating Eugene V. Debs's power as head of the American Railway Union. Drawing from Harper's Weekly.

CHAPTER SIX

"Just an Old Woman"

MARY AND OTHER UNION MEMBERS refused to be discouraged by the opposition they faced. One of Mary's friends, Eugene V. Debs, was particularly courageous. Debs was a railroad worker from Indiana who was determined to improve conditions for the men who kept America's trains running.

The railroad workers were organized into several small unions according to particular skills or crafts. The electrical workers, for instance, belonged to a union that was separate from the porters, and the brakemen belonged to yet another union. When one group went out on strike, other groups remained on the job. And the trains still ran.

Debs saw the need for a broader union that would include all rail workers and provide more clout against the owners. In 1893, he formed the American Railway Union, uniting the various unions into one powerful group. When they won one strike against the Great Northern Railroad, they turned their attention to the Pullman works. Once again, Chicago was the site of the action.

After the Great Chicago Fire, George Pullman had built the Pullman Palace Car Company in a suburb south of Chicago. He named the town after himself. The town included the plant and houses and shops for the company's workers and their families. Pullman boasted of his community as a model for working communities everywhere, but his employees saw it differently.

The houses were owned by Pullman, and the rent charged to the workers was deducted from their paychecks. When another depression hit the country in the 1890s, Pullman cut his workers' wages and raised their rents.

Some workers had only pennies left in their paychecks at the end of each week. In despair the workers formed a committee to take their grievances to Pullman. He refused to meet with them and fired three of the committee's members.

Eugene Debs and the 150,000 members of his union took up the cause of the Pullman workers and called a strike that shut down the entire nation's railroads. Again, federal troops were called in to stop the strike. In Chicago in the summer of 1894, members of the United States army confronted ARU strikers in Chicago. In the violence that followed, several strikers were killed and others wounded. Debs was arrested and put in jail. The rail workers returned to their jobs defeated. The same old conditions existed. Wages remained low and many of the strikers were blacklisted.

By now, Mary had thrown herself wholeheartedly into America's labor movement. In her autobiography she mentions being involved in many of the early labor strikes, but she probably did not play a very large role. But as time went on she began to gain the reputation as a dramatic speaker and effective union organizer.

In 1895, together with her friend Julius Wayland, she started a publication called *Appeal to Reason*, which was a magazine that told the stories of the country's workers and urged them into action. Mary's role was to sell subscriptions to the magazine, a job she undertook with enthusiasm since she was a firm believer in education.

"I have always advised men to read," she wrote in her autobiography. "All my life I have told them to study the works of those great authors who have been interested in making this world a happier place for those who do its drudgery. . . . 'Boys,' I would say, 'listen to me. Instead of going to the pool or gambling rooms, go up to the mountain and read this book.'"

Mary's promotion of *Appeal to Reason* took her to Birmingham,

Railway workers refused to service these elegant dining cars during the Pullman strike of 1894.

Alabama, where coal miners and rail workers were out on strike. Women in the labor movement were rare, and women in the coal fields were even rarer. It must have shocked the miners to see a middle-aged lady in a black dress buttonholing reluctant miners at the mine entrance. Mary was now in her fifties and was such a force that the local militia, which was trying to squelch the union's efforts to organize, told Mary she could not hold meetings or give speeches.

"I was forbidden to hold meetings," she wrote later. "Nevertheless I slipped through the ranks of the soldiers without their knowing who I was—just an old woman going to a missionary meeting to knit mittens for the heathens of Africa." Once past the militia she traveled to a nearby mining camp and held her meeting anyway.

Mary was still in Alabama when Eugene Debs was released from jail in 1896. He scheduled a rally for the railroad workers and their sympathizers at the opera house in Birmingham. Announcements went up all over town and the workers of the city were excited about his arrival. But local officials issued an injunction, or order, saying that the meeting could not be held, and they warned the owner of the opera house not to open his doors for the meeting.

Mary and the other labor organizers in town rose to the challenge. They brought in miners from nearby towns for a rally at the local union hall. Just before Debs's train was due to arrive at the station Mary marched several thousand miners to the depot.

"The train pulled in and Debs got off," she wrote. "Those miners did not wait for the gates to open but jumped over the railing. They put him on their shoulders and marched out of the station with the crowd in line. They marched through the streets, past the railway offices, the mayor's office, the office of the chief of police. 'Debs is here! Debs is here!' they shouted."

The doors of the opera house miraculously opened and the throng held its meeting in spite of town opposition. "The churches were empty that night," she wrote, "and that night the crowd heard a real sermon by a preacher whose message was one of human brotherhood."

CHAPTER SEVEN

Miners' Angel

W HEN MARY BEGAN HER WORK as a labor organizer in the coal
fields of Pennsylvania in the late 1890s she was known as Mary
Harris Jones. When she left a few years later, she had earned the de-
votion of the coal miners and was known as Mother Jones.

The miners loved her because she believed they deserved a better life
and she was willing to risk her comfort—and in some cases her life—to
help them gain it. When they lacked the courage to strike, she led them
into battle. They called her the "miners' angel."

The miners needed an angel. Their conditions were dangerous and
their wages low. In an attempt to better their conditions the Knights of
Labor had formed the United Mine Workers of America (UMWA) in
1890. Members staged a large but not very successful strike in 1894.
Mary was not involved in that strike, but three years later she was on
the scene with miners in the Pittsburgh area. A labor newspaper reported that "Mrs. Mary Jones of Chicago . . . has done more missionary work for the miners . . . than any two officials and done it better.
To her, more than to anyone else, the miners owe much of their success. . . . She has roughed it in this district for four weeks in all kinds of
weather."

In 1899 Mary arrived in Arnot, Pennsylvania, to help with a strike

Young miners ready to enter the coal tunnel for what might be a twelve-hour day. Photo by Lewis Hine.

OPPOSITE: *A United Mine Workers' membership certificate calling for "an earning fully compatible with the dangers of our calling": an end to scrip, safer mines, an eight-hour day, and an end to child labor.*

that had been in progress for several months. By October the men were ready to admit defeat and go back to work, but Mary changed all that.

When she arrived, she stayed in a hotel in town where she thought she was welcome. But the place was owned by the coal company. When they discovered she was there to organize the miners, she was told to leave. A miner's family then took her into their little home, where the husband insisted that she sleep in the bedroom while he slept sitting in a chair in the kitchen. But the company owned the miner's house, too, and the whole family was soon evicted and out on the street.

Immigrant miners' wives look for coal on a dump during a Pennsylvania coal strike.

That event, Mary reported, was a turning point. When the other townspeople saw Mary, the miner, his wife, and his children walking through town with their belongings looking for a safe place to stay, they were so angry they resolved to stay out on strike rather than give in.

Within days, Mary had organized the miners' wives and marched a colorful parade of women carrying mops and brooms to the mines. They shouted at the scabs and banged noisily on their pots and pans.

"I selected as a leader an Irish woman who had a most picturesque appearance," Mary wrote years later. "She had slept late and her husband had told her to hurry up and get into the army. She had grabbed a red petticoat and slipped it over a thick cotton night gown. She wore a black stocking and a white one. She had tied a little red fringed shawl over her wild red hair. Her face was red and her eyes were mad. I looked at her and felt that she could raise a rumpus."

Mary told her, "Take that tin dishpan you have with you and your hammer and when the scabs and the mules come up begin to hammer and howl."

The woman and her followers did just that and when the mine superintendent protested, she "took the old tin pan and she hit him with it and she hollered, 'To hell with you and the mules!'"

As Mary told it, the man fell over into a creek and the mules and the scabs bolted. Then, she said, the "scabs started running down hill, followed by the army of women with their mops and pails and brooms." Perhaps Mary exaggerated the drama, but it was certain that she had learned how to get attention.

Throughout the strike, Mary held meetings to rally the spirits of the miners. She traveled by wagon with a miner's son as her driver. It was sometimes midnight or one in the morning when they reached home with Mary driving and the boy asleep on her arm. "Sometimes it was several degrees below zero . . . my hands and feet were often numb," she wrote. "We were all living on dry bread and black coffee."

By February of 1900, the Arnot strike was won and the men returned to their jobs with a pay increase. To celebrate, the miners held a giant

President Theodore Roosevelt and the committee formed to settle the 1902 coal strike. Mother Jones thought the union could have demanded a better settlement.

rally in Blossburg, a nearby town. Many of the men walked miles through the bitter cold to pay tribute to Mother Jones. The celebration lasted all night and the "dear little children," as she later referred to them, kissed her hand. The miners also presented her with a gold watch, but she turned it down, thinking the money could be better spent feeding the miners' families.

During those early years as an organizer, Mother Jones held great respect for leaders of the United Mine Workers. One of her favorites was Douglass Wilson. He, like others she admired, endured the same hardships as the striking miners. He provided housing for miners in his barn when they were evicted from their company-owned houses, and killed his chickens and hogs to provide them with food. "He knew every hardship that the rank and file of the organization knew," she wrote.

She was not so complimentary of John Mitchell, who became the union's national president. Mitchell gave Mother Jones her first job as a union organizer for the UMWA in 1900, and initially she admired him. But she was bitterly disappointed when President Theodore Roosevelt persuaded him to allow the federal government to arbitrate the disagreements of the 1902 coal strike.

The striking miners had shut down so many mines that the country's businesses and homes were suffering acutely from lack of fuel. The miners had enough clout to win whatever demands they made. But according to Mother Jones, Mitchell caved in to the demands of the mine owners because he was flattered by the attention he got from the President.

During these early years in the coal fields Mother Jones was making a name for herself. A reporter covering the Pennsylvania strike warned John Mitchell that "Mother Jones is up in the mountains raising hell with a bunch of wild women."

Indeed she was. And having learned a thing or two about how to do it, she was ready now to turn her attention to rallying the miners in West Virginia.

Work in the mines required the help of mules. Photo by Lewis Hine.

CHAPTER EIGHT

Coal Wars in West Virginia

WEST VIRGINIA WAS THE COAL UNION'S toughest challenge. Naturally Mother Jones loved it. She spent years there tramping its remote gullies and hollows, rounding up miners and preaching the gospel of unionism.

When Mother Jones first came to the state in the late 1890s, West Virginia miners were the most poorly paid in the country. They dug a large portion of the coal used by the country's trains, factories, and homes, but they were paid much less than miners in other states.

The mines were dangerous, dark, and lonely. Roof cave-ins and explosions were common. Mines had only one portal, or entrance, so if there was an accident the men were trapped with no alternate way out. The work shifts were long—ten, sometimes twelve hours a day. For this dangerous, backbreaking work, a miner received less than three hundred dollars a year.

West Virginia miners should have been eager to join the union. With more than twenty thousand miners in the state, there were enough to challenge the mine owners for better pay and conditions. But the companies had total control over the miners.

The companies owned everything—the mines, the land around them, the miners' houses, and the only stores in the area. They also owned the roads leading to and from the mining communities as well

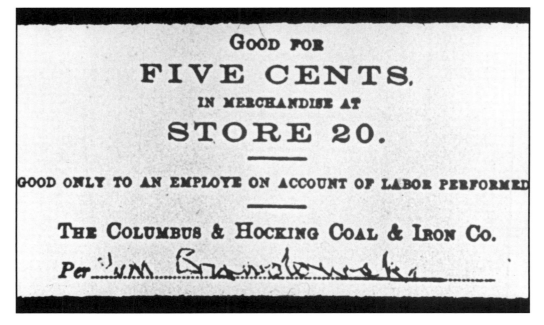

Miners received scrip like this, not money, for their work in the mines.

as the schools and the churches. The doctors, teachers, and ministers were all paid and controlled by the coal operators.

Miners were paid in scrip, certificates that could be exchanged for food and other goods at the company store. Often by the end of the month a miner was actually in debt to the company.

Mother Jones told of a miner whose family she stayed with who owed ten tons of coal for rent, two for drinking water, two for the doctor, and so on. The weighman who tallied up the number of tons mined by each man each day was a company official and miners often felt they were being cheated.

Since all the buildings in their communities were owned by the company, the miners had no place to hold union meetings. Organizing was further complicated because the miners' homes were isolated from one another by steep mountains and gullies.

The miners wanted an eight-hour day, better wages, and their own weighman. But the operators did everything they could to keep the miners from forming a union.

By controlling the local court system, the mine owners made sure that local judges shared their anti-union sentiment. Judges were quite

Half Month Ending _____ *1/31/[ ]_____ No. _165_

Mr. _____*Herbert Ramsey*_____

BALANCE DUE WORKMAN $_____

LAUREL SMOKELESS COAL CO.

By	Tons	Cwt.			To Store Account		18	01
"	"	*13*	"		8	86	" Balance	13	90
"	Yards	@		6	00	" Rent		
"	"	@				" Coal		
"	Slate					" Smithing		07
"	Days	@				" Labor		21
"	"	@				" Cash Advanced		
" Month's Salary					" Doctor		
" Cks. Returned					" Burial Fund		10
" Labor	@				" Checks		
					" Insurance		
Cash held last day to Balance				" Hospital		
Account					" Lights		
					Check off		50
					O. A. P.		14
					U. I.		
Total Earnings	14	86		Total Debit	33	41
By Balance Due Workman				To Bal. Due Co.	18	55

- -

Received of   No._____

LAUREL SMOKELESS COAL COMPANY

DOLLARS		in full of all claims to and including
CENTS		

Witness at Signing _____

Sign Here _____
Paragon Print. 2M 9-38 100884

LIABLE FOR ANY SUBSEQUENT INDEBTEDNESS

A company worksheet shows a miner owing the company rather than receiving pay.

willing to issue injunctions, legal orders that prohibited union organizers from speaking and holding meetings. "In West Virginia you
can't step on a piece of ground without you step on an injunction,"
Mother Jones told a newspaper reporter.

If miners were bold enough to go to a union meeting, they were often
evicted from their company-owned houses and arrested. Sometimes
they were deported, or sent out of the state and told not to return.
Blacklisting was also common. When miners did strike, the company
hired scabs from outside the area to take the jobs of striking miners.

Mother Jones was in West Virginia when the United Mine Workers
and leaders from other unions decided it was time for an all-out effort
to organize the state. There had been strikes in the state before but they
had failed and the coal union had few members.

None of this discouraged Mother Jones. In typical fashion, she took
on the toughest part of the state to organize, the rough, isolated Paint
Creek region. Since she was not able to post notices for meetings, she
used ingenious methods for spreading the word. Once she sent two
men into a coal camp. "One pretended he was deaf and the other kept
hollering in his ear as they walked around, 'Mother Jones is going to
have a meeting Sunday afternoon outside the town on the sawdust
pile.' Then the deaf fellow would ask him what he said and he would
holler to him again. So the word got around the entire camp and we had
a big crowd."

The miners in West Virginia loved her fiery speeches and her will-
ingness to go everywhere. She was fearless and energetic in tramping
the rifle-filled hills. In a letter to John Mitchell, president of the
UMWA, she told of having sore bones from having to slide down a
mountain and of getting home late at night from an organizing meeting. The hours were long and many nights she was out in the mountains
past midnight. Since hotels were owned by the coal companies, she
usually stayed in one of the miners' shacks. Her pay in 1900 from the
United Mine Workers was just under five hundred dollars.

"Frequently," she said, "we would hear bullets whizz past us as we
sat huddled between boulders, our black clothes making us invisible in
the blackness of the night."

"MOTHER" JONES TALKS TO MINERS ON CABIN CREEK, AND STRIKE WILL FOLLOW

OBNOXIOUS GUARDS FROM PAINT CREEK WERE TRANSFERRED TO CABIN CREEK— TROUBLE THERE SO ON FOLLOWED—BOOMER TROUBLES ARE PRACTICALLY SETTLED— 6,000 MEN ARE STILL ON STRIKE

CHARLESTON, August 11.—Growing out of the strike of coal miners on Paint creek, which has been on since the middle of last April, is an organized movement having for its purpose the organization of all coal miners in West Virginia for a general strike. Definite information to this effect has been received by State officials though the operators in fields now without apparent strike troubles declare it unfounded, while the officials of the union miners only partially admit it.

With the exception of a part of the Knawha field and the northern Panhandle the miners of the state are not known members of the union. Where the miners are organized muchtrouble was experienced in agreeing upon a new scale when the old agree-ment expired April first. Agreements were finally reached at practically all the mines except Paint creek, in the Kanawha field, where about one-fifthof the full force is now working. The entire state militia, with the exception of two companies which are on duty at Peytona and Sterling, is on duty on Paint creek. The Peytona and Sterling troubles have been settled and tomorrow the militia there will return home, one company to Charleston and the other to Kingwood.

Taking advantage of the Paint Creek situation the organizers for the United Mine Workers of America have been attempting to effect an organization wherever coal is mined in the state. How far they have succeeded is kept from the public. It is definitely known, however, that they have gone far enough to threaten a State-wide strike, whether the miners really have joined the union or not. The operators, generally, in the state are uneasy though they declare there is nochance of such a strike. There is apparent a feeling of unrest among theminers, notwithstanding in many sections they are making more money thanever before.

The demand of the miners on Paint creek, if conceded, would give them an increase of from two to two and one-half cents per ton. About fifteen hundred miners are on strike there but, according to the strikers themselves, their main grievance now is the treatment received by them at the

In 1902 Mother Jones was in West Virginia for a state-wide strike. Sixteen thousand miners walked off their jobs when the coal operators refused to meet their demands for higher wages and the right to join the union. Again the operators went all out to keep the coal fields non-union.

Mother Jones got a first-hand look at the operators' violence on one of her nighttime treks when she found a wounded miner who had been beaten and left in the road. She bandaged his head with strips torn from her petticoat. Then, to fool the attackers into fleeing, she yelled out, "Don't worry. The boys are on their way."

Mother Jones knew she risked being arrested when she scheduled a speech in Clarksburg to rally the miners. She went ahead with plans anyway and thousands of handbills were posted to announce the event. She had spoken for only thirty minutes, barely a warm-up for her, when she was arrested. She was charged with violating an injunction and taken to court.

Indignant, she called the judge a scab, the highest insult she could think of. He responded by lecturing her to stay home, then released her on bail. He later said he found her a woman of great intelligence and was puzzled as to why she would choose such a rough, unwomanly life. He refused, however, to allow her to "force her way into jail." The judge knew that behind bars she would gain considerable sympathy and publicity for the miners' cause.

Mother Jones often swore profusely in her speeches and she adapted her speaking style to suit whatever audience she encountered. With immigrants she often used an odd blend of broken English, a smattering of foreign phrases, and plenty of swear words. Her message always

Mother Jones rallies miners at a speech in West Virginia.

A cartoon showing a miner's surprise at seeing sunlight.

came through loud and clear, though: Join the union and fight for your rights.

She used her age and the fact that she was a woman to benefit her cause. The striking miners were not so lucky. In a coal camp on Stanford Mountain a group of miners held a meeting near mine property to talk about joining the union and a deputy marshal came to arrest them. When the miners fought back, the company sent an eighty-man posse to the village at four A.M. When they left, seven men were dead, shot as they lay sleeping.

Mother Jones went immediately to comfort the miners' widows and children and to encourage the miners to continue the strike. The miners persevered and by the end of the strike they had won a shorter work day and the right to shop at stores not owned by the company. And they were now free to join the union.

With Mother Jones's help the miners achieved a real victory. It was a victory that did not last long, however, and several years later she was back in West Virginia lending a hand to "her boys." But now she was ready to turn her attention to the textile workers and bring the nation's attention to the cause of children laboring in the mills.

Mother Jones lamented the plight of children who changed spindles in the textile mills. Photo by Lewis Hine.

CHAPTER NINE

A March for the Children

NOTHING MOVED MOTHER JONES more than the plight of working children. She had heard the stories of little hands caught in the shuttles of the textile looms, of five-year-old children filing off to work before dawn, and of young women whose lungs were ruined by the lint and dust in the mills.

Mother Jones had seen child labor first hand when she traveled through Alabama in 1895. When she had applied for a job in a cotton mill in Cottondale, the manager told her he could not hire her unless she had a family who would work with her. In what must have been a painful reminder of her life in Memphis, he asked her if she had children. "Yes," she told him. "There are six of us." This twisting of the truth earned her a job at the mill and the privilege of renting a rundown shanty with broken windows and a rotten floor. The children, she promised the manager, would be arriving from another town soon.

Meanwhile, she began work and there "saw the children, little children working, the most heart-rending spectacle in all life." She saw boys and girls walking up and down the rows of spindles and reaching their little hands into the machinery to fix threads that had snapped loose.

"They crawled under machinery to oil it. They replaced spindles all day long, all night long; night through, night through. Tiny babies of

Two young girls at work in a textile factory. Photo by Lewis Hine.

six years old with faces of sixty did an eight-hour shift for ten cents a day." Four-year-olds came to the mills to help older brothers and sisters. They, however, received no pay.

Mother Jones discovered that sleep was very important to these children. Up before dawn, they filed into the factory at 5:30 A.M. and worked till their half-hour lunch break. Many of them fell asleep on the floor instead of having their noon meal. At night they were often too tired to eat and fell into bed to sleep, "the one happiness these children know."

In Selma, Alabama, Mother Jones took a job in another mill and lived with a woman whose eleven-year-old daughter Maggie worked there too. In her book she told the story of friends coming by on Sunday to get Maggie to go with them for an outing. Maggie was still in bed.

" 'Oh Mother,' she said, 'just let me sleep; that's a lot more fun. I'm so tired I just want to sleep forever.'

"So," Mary reported, "her mother let her sleep. The next day she went as usual to the mill. That evening at four o'clock they brought her home and laid her tiny body on the kitchen table. She was asleep—forever. Her hair had caught in the machinery and torn her scalp off."

The South was not the only home of child labor. When she was in Pennsylvania helping to organize the coal workers, Mother Jones learned that the miners' wives worked at the nearby silk factories. Because most families could not survive on just the mothers' and fathers' salaries, their daughters worked in the mills too. The sons worked as "breaker boys" in mine sheds sorting slate from coal.

At the turn of the century, there were more than two million children under the age of sixteen employed in mines, mills, and factories in the United States. In the South, as Mary had discovered, adults had to have children who could work in order to get a job. In the North, where some states had laws against child labor, many parents lied about their children's ages so they could help out with the family's income.

Twenty-eight states actually had laws to protect children, but they were not enforced and offered little protection anyway. In Pennsylva-

Breaker boys, some as young as six, sort coal. Photo by Frances B. Johnson.

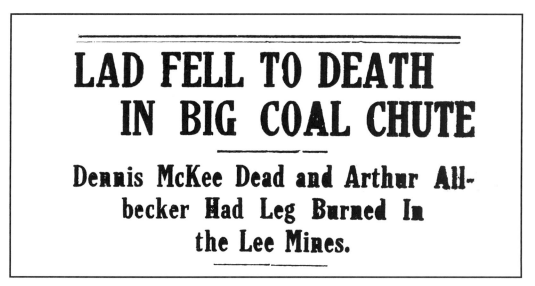

LAD FELL TO DEATH IN BIG COAL CHUTE

Dennis McKee Dead and Arthur All- becker Had Leg Burned In the Lee Mines.

A newspaper report of a boy killed in a coal mine accident.

nia, for instance, the law required that a working child be at least thirteen years old and work no more than ten hours a day, six days a week. In reality, many children in the textile mills were much younger. Their average pay was two dollars per week. Accidents involving children were common.

In Kensington, Pennsylvania, mill workers went on strike in 1903 to

A young boy pushes a coal cart through the mine tunnel.

gain better conditions. When Mother Jones traveled there to urge on the strikers she found little support in the community for the workers' cause. What was needed, she decided, was some dramatic event to focus public attention on the plight of the striking textile workers.

Mother Jones thought child labor was a national disgrace, and a national disgrace required national action. Teddy Roosevelt, America's progressive president, was spending the summer at Sagamore Hills, his vacation home on New York's Long Island. Mary decided to organize a grand parade of textile workers from Pennsylvania to Long Island. Her plan was for the march to end with a visit to Roosevelt's doorstep, demanding that he sponsor a federal law to end child labor.

Almost one hundred children received permission from their parents to go on Mother Jones's march. Another two hundred adult strikers set out with them. Mother Jones rode in one of the wagons.

A Pennsylvania boy whose leg was crushed between rail cars in a coal mine. Photo by Lewis Hine.

A fife and drum corps, playing "Marching Through Georgia," led the marchers out of Kensington, and a small boy carried a sign that read, "We Are Textile Workers." The wagons were draped in red, white, and blue bunting. The marchers' spirits were high after an enthusiastic sendoff in town.

The first night out they camped at a picnic ground and raised more than seventy dollars from interested bystanders. From there on they were plagued with scorching temperatures, heavy rains, and mosquitoes. Most of the women dropped out after a few days and some of the children returned home, too, when the heat became too much for them to bear.

The remaining marchers were a colorful if sometimes bedraggled sight. They paraded northward, stopping in towns along the way. They drew attention everywhere and, much to Mother Jones's delight, the newspapers sent reporters to cover the event.

A Philadelphia newspaper called her "the greatest female agitator in the country." A reporter for the *New York World* quoted her as saying that the marchers would "parade up and down Wall Street to show the millionaires the little emaciated boys and overworked men who have earned their millions for them."

Not all the coverage was favorable, though. One unhappy striker told a *New York Times* reporter: "It's all right for Mother Jones . . . she sleeps in a hotel. I would rather work sixty hours a day than to endure this torture. We seem to be a kind of side show to help her get some notoriety about the country."

There was probably some truth in what the striker told the reporter, for certainly Mother Jones loved being in the limelight. She was in her element as the leader of the march.

She spoke eloquently, and at great length, at their roadside rallies and raised money for their cause. In one town, when the first round of contributions did not raise enough to suit her, she scolded the audience and passed the hat again. In Princeton, New Jersey, home of the prestigious university, she railed against the money students were spending on education. It ought to go to organized labor, she said. She spoke in front of the university and pointed to one of the boys who worked in the textile mill. "Here's a textbook on economics," she said. "He gets three dollars a week and his sister, who is fourteen, gets six."

By the time the marchers were ready to cross the river from New Jersey into New York City, many had returned home. Mother Jones's enthusiasm and creativity never flagged, however. When the New York City police chief told her the group could not get a permit to parade through the streets, she met with the city's mayor. A group of visiting Chinese dignitaries had recently been entertained by the mayor at city expense. If the mayor could do that for "foreigners," he certainly could grant a parade permit to his own country's workers, Mother Jones told him. The mayor gave in and granted the permit.

The group paraded north from the lower part of Manhattan and listened as Mother Jones delivered a streetcorner speech. Local shop girls and businessmen looked on curiously. The next day, the boys in the group swam in the East River while the men shot pool at a local billiards hall.

Later in the week Mother Jones led the group to Madison Square Garden, where she planned to present a great show with dramas performed by the children. They were again stopped by a policeman who told them they did not have a proper permit. Undaunted, Mother Jones made friends with the policeman, marched arm in arm with him to a nearby intersection, and there delivered an hour-long speech. When she finished, she had gathered a cheering crowd of almost two thousand who blocked the subway entrance and held up the noonday flow of traffic. But the rally at Madison Square Garden never did take place.

From New York City the marchers moved on to Coney Island, the amusement park on Long Island. The owner of a wild animal show there offered them a few days of free lodging and entertainment. While the children swam in the Atlantic Ocean, Mother Jones prepared for an afternoon speech.

With her usual flair for drama, Mother Jones had the children on stage, peering out from behind the bars of the empty animal cages. The children were imprisoned in their jobs, she told the crowd, much as the animals were in their cages. While she spoke, several lions nearby began to roar and drowned out part of her speech.

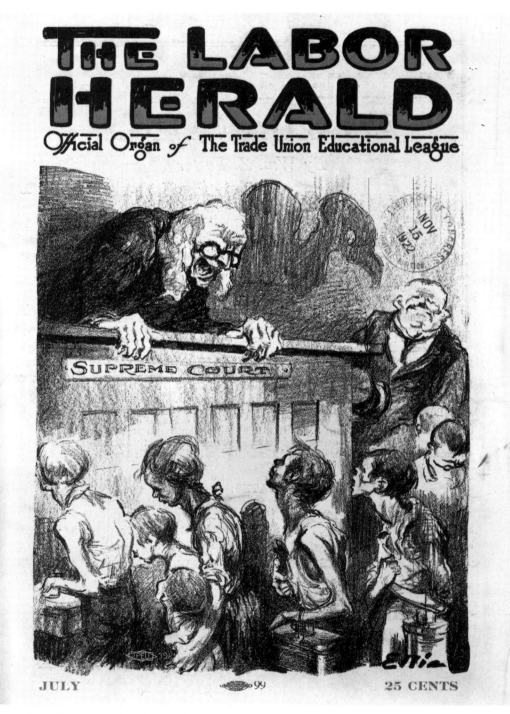

A political cartoon lambasts the Supreme Court for finding a federal law prohibiting child labor unconstitutional.

Later, she found out that United States Senator Thomas Platt was staying at a hotel nearby. With Mother Jones in the lead, the group marched on the senator's hotel seeking his support for their cause. But he slipped out the back door, desperate to avoid confronting the determined old lady and her followers. When the marchers discovered he had escaped them, Mother Jones led the children through the hotel's kitchen, sat them down at the tables in the hotel's restaurant, ordered breakfast for them—and charged it all to the senator's bill.

By now, Mother Jones and the remaining marchers were within a day's walk of President Roosevelt's estate. Mother Jones had sent two letters to the President from points along the march, but his secretary wrote back saying the President could meet with her only if she set up a regular appointment at the White House. Secret Servicemen who thought she might be a threat to the President had followed Mother Jones throughout the march. Now they came to her and told her it was not a good idea to continue the march.

Mother Jones would not cave in, but she did scale back on her original idea of taking all the marchers to Roosevelt's home. Perhaps she thought she might look ridiculous. She chose three boys and two adults and quietly proceeded to Sagamore Hills. The President's secretary met them outside the gate and told them that the President would not meet with them. Defeated, Mother Jones and her followers boarded a train back to Manhattan.

Mother Jones told reporters that she would organize a march to Washington to gain support from Congress. But she received a letter from the President saying that Congress did not have the power to act on the child labor issue. The matter was up to each state, he said. The march was over and the children went back to the mills.

The end to the march was a letdown for the mill workers and a disappointment to Mother Jones. What the march did accomplish was to make Mother Jones a national figure. She was a champion of the working poor who knew how to get publicity for her causes. When the marchers returned to the Pennsylvania mills they had to endure the same dismal conditions as before. Mother Jones headed west to Colorado and the fight that awaited her there.

The United Mine Workers of America announces its effort to organize Colorado workers.

CHAPTER TEN

The "Good Fight Against Wrong"

A UNITED STATES CONGRESSMAN one time asked Mother Jones where she resided. She replied, "I reside wherever there is a good fight against wrong—all over the country." And, true to her word, when the 1903 march of the mill children was over, she moved on to Colorado to help the miners there.

The governor and other officials in Colorado did not want unions in their state and did everything they could to keep the miners from organizing. Officials from the United Mine Workers sent Mother Jones to the state to check out the situation.

Since she did not want to be recognized, she disguised herself as a peddler. "I got myself an old calico dress," she wrote later, "a sunbonnet, some pins and needles, elastic and tape and such sundries, and went down to the southern coal fields of the Colorado Fuel and Iron Company."

In her visits with the miners she found their conditions "deplorable." As in West Virginia, the companies owned the miners' houses, all the land, the schools, and the churches. Men were paid in scrip, and if they did not shop at company stores, they were fired. The coal they mined was weighed by company weighmen, and the miners were frequently cheated. Their days were long.

Mother Jones was galled that Colorado miners were living in poverty on sixty-three cents a day while the president of the union, John

A group of immigrant Colorado miners' wives and children. Many did not speak English.

The families of evicted Colorado miners lived in tents and cooked outside.

Mitchell, was vacationing in Europe and staying at expensive hotels. She always felt that union officers should not live better than the workers they represented. She was openly critical of Mitchell, but he knew she was one of his best organizers and kept sending her into difficult areas. Colorado was one such place.

Trinidad, Walsenburg, and Ludlow were tiny mining towns in southern Colorado. The towns were dominated by the Victor Fuel Company and the Colorado Fuel and Iron Company, which was owned by the family of John D. Rockefeller, Sr. He was one of the country's wealthiest and most powerful men and a frequent target of Mother Jones's criticism. Most miners at the Rockefeller operations were immigrants from Greece, Italy, and Mexico, isolated from each other by language as well as by the Colorado mountains.

In the northern part of the state the workers were already union members. Miners there had walked off their jobs in November, 1903, and had gained an eight-hour day and higher pay. But the southern miners had not been included in the contract and their wages and conditions remained pitiful. They stayed out on strike and the company

Colorado tent communities offered little protection from the cold.

evicted them from their houses and brought in scab laborers to take their jobs in the mines.

Mother Jones went to be with the miners and as usual she refused any kind of luxury. She spent much of her time with the miners in their freezing, snow-covered tents in the mountains. By January, 1904, she was in the hospital with pneumonia.

When she was able she returned to the striking miners. But company guards put her on a train out of the state, telling her she was under orders from the governor not to return to Colorado.

Mary always had friends who worked on the trains and she talked the conductor into taking her to Denver. She then checked into a hotel and wrote the governor a letter saying: "I am right here in the capital . . . four or five blocks from your office. What in Hell are you going to do about it?" Before he could do much she was on her way to Utah to help organize the miners there.

In Utah, the mine owners used a different tactic to keep her from organizing. When she tried to hold meetings, the mine guards spread the word that she had been exposed to smallpox and must be quarantined. They locked her in a shack at the edge of town, but mysteriously the shack burned to the ground and she was rescued.

Soon she was back in Colorado, where she saw numerous violations of the miners' rights as United States citizens. Guards put miners and their families in bullpens and held them there as prisoners. Union organizers' homes were bombed. Shopkeepers and ministers were told not to support the strikers. The tent cities were raided, and men were sent out of the state on trains and ordered not to return.

Mother Jones wanted action from President Theodore Roosevelt and called him a coward for not sending troops to restore order in Colorado. Roosevelt refused, however, and soon the southern Colorado miners, weary from fighting a battle it seemed they could not win, returned to work defeated.

While she was in Colorado the mine companies tried to ruin Mother Jones's reputation by planting a story about her past in a Denver gossip newspaper called *Polly Pry*. The story claimed she had run a house of prostitution in Denver years earlier. The article was circulated to other

Mother Jones poses with miners' families in southern Colorado.

newspapers—mostly in areas where she went as an organizer. Terrance Powderly and others of her friends were outraged by the article, but Mother Jones never bothered to comment on it. She just went on organizing.

When the strike in southern Colorado failed, Mother Jones felt that both the government and the union had failed the miners. The UMWA

Striking Colorado miners tough it out in tents during one of the state's worst blizzards.

was no longer feisty enough to suit her, so she resigned and joined the more radical Socialist party.

Radicals were gaining strength in the labor movement, and in 1905 several leaders, discontent with existing unions, met in Chicago. Mother Jones was one of the founders of the new group, which called itself the Industrial Workers of the World (IWW). It was a radical group representing immigrants, migrant workers, lumberjacks, farmers, and factory workers. The IWW wanted to overthrow the country's business system and turn the mines, railroads, and other businesses over to the government. As the organization grew, however, Mother Jones found she did not agree with its goals and she had little to do with the group she had helped to found.

During the next few years, Mother Jones traveled the length and breadth of the country helping the copper workers in Michigan and Arizona, the telegraph workers in Chicago, and the shirtwaist workers in New York City.

Once, while she was in the West, she became involved in international politics. Porfirio Díaz, president of Mexico at that time, was anti-union and had little sympathy for the working class. A group of revolutionaries were planning to overthrow his government and had taken refuge in the United States. One was kidnapped by United States officials and sent back to Mexico to jail. Others were arrested, beaten, and sent to jail in California.

Mother Jones witnessed the kidnapping in Douglas, Arizona, in 1907 and immediately took up the cause of the Mexican revolutionaries. The United States government should provide protection for people fleeing from repressive governments, she thought, and she sent telegrams to President Roosevelt and raised money for the men's defense.

In 1909, her old friend Terrance Powderly arranged for her to meet with President William Taft and she pleaded for the Mexican prisoners' release. Mother Jones became a great heroine to these men. Later, when Díaz was overthrown, she went to Mexico to meet with the new president, Francisco Madero, who was pro-union and wanted her to help organize the Mexican miners.

In 1910 the women working in the beer breweries in Milwaukee asked Mother Jones to come help them organize a union. Of course she went. She published several articles telling of the women's poor wages and working conditions. Then she asked her old friends in the UMWA to support the strikers by boycotting Milwaukee beer. She also planned to get state legislators to pass a law prohibiting the hiring of women in the breweries. Soon the owners of the breweries accepted the demands of the strikers and the women were back at work with higher wages, better conditions, and the right to join the union.

It was also in 1910 that Mother Jones orchestrated one of her more colorful protests. She was visiting strikers in Pennsylvania and there she urged a group of miners' wives to sing themselves out of jail. They had picketed the mines to harass some scabs who were filling their husbands' jobs at the mines. They had their babies in their arms when they were arrested and sent to jail.

Mother Jones, knowing a good tactic when she saw one, encouraged the women to sing to their babies all night long at the top of their lungs. They did, and made life so miserable for those in the surrounding houses that the judge sourly let them go free after five days.

All this activity might have tired any other person, but Mother Jones seemed to thrive on it. After all, she was doing what she believed in the most—providing a voice for those who had no voice. She had done more in the last few years than most people do in a lifetime. But her most dramatic fights were yet to come.

West Virginia militia at a coal mine.

CHAPTER ELEVEN

"I Didn't Come Out on a Stretcher"

MOTHER JONES was in Montana when she heard of new union troubles in West Virginia. She immediately canceled speaking engagements she had scheduled in San Francisco, tied up all her possessions in a black shawl—"I like traveling light," she wrote—and headed for "her boys."

When she arrived in the state in the summer of 1912, she climbed the capitol steps in Charleston and, in a two-hour speech, excited the miners to a fever pitch. If the operators had held any doubt before, they now knew that the strike was on and was likely to be a bloody one.

Mother Jones often said she detested violence and never actively encouraged it. After her speech, however, more than a thousand rifles were sold in the city.

The scene of the strike was the part of the state Mary thought she had left organized several years earlier. Union miners, including those in the tiny community of Paint Creek, had walked off the job because their new contract did not include the improvements they were seeking. Across the deep ravine from Paint Creek the Cabin Creek miners remained nonunion and were afraid to join in the strike.

The seventeen-mile valley that separated the two towns was controlled by the mine companies. The companies had hired guards from the Baldwin-Felts Detective Agency, a group of professional thugs armed with rifles, clubs, and machine guns. No union organizers dared go into the area. Union officials told Mother Jones that if she went there she would "come out on a stretcher."

Nearby was Eskdale, known as a "free town" because it was not controlled by the coal operators. Mother Jones used her friends who worked on the railroads to spread the word that she would hold a meeting there.

She spoke to the Paint Creek and Cabin Creek miners and encouraged them to fight violence with violence. During one speech she even held up a mine guard's uniform, full of bullet holes and caked with dried blood. This, she announced, was the first such uniform she had seen that was decorated to suit her. She then ripped up the uniform and threw pieces of it to the audience as souvenirs.

By now the operators were calling Mother Jones a "busybody" from outside the area, "creating dissatisfaction" where none had existed before. Up until her arrival, they claimed, the miners of Cabin Creek had been content and taken pride in their "honest labor" in the coal mines.

Miners from Red Warrior, a nearby town, came to Mother Jones and asked her to come to their town to help unionize the men. To get there, she had to drive a buggy through a creek bed while the men walked along the railroad track. While she was driving she heard bullets whizzing past and the miners screaming. She ran to them and found them huddled together around the bend from a bunch of mine guards with a machine gun.

The way she told the story later, Mother Jones walked up to the gunman, put her hand on the muzzle of the machine gun, and told him not to shoot. When the guards continued to threaten her she told them, "If you touch one of my white hairs that creek will run with blood, and yours will be the first to crimson it." She told them she had five hundred miners hiding in the hills behind her and they were ready to shoot as soon as she gave the word. The guards gave in and the miners marched past the machine gun and continued on through the hills to their meeting.

Baldwin-Felts mine guards with their rifles.

Back in Charleston again, Mother Jones delivered another long-winded speech, declaring the miners would "buy every gun in Charleston" if the mine guard system was not abolished.

By now both the miners and the company guards had so many guns and so much ammunition that the state was virtually at war. Governor

Ammunition, rifles, and machine guns stockpiled during the 1912-13 West Virginia coal strike.

West Virginia militia arrest evicted coal miners.

William E. Glasscock declared martial law. Miners were arrested and punished, sometimes even shot, without being officially charged with a crime or given a trial. When the governor sent state troops into the Cabin Creek area, they seized almost two thousand rifles, more than five hundred pistols, six machine guns, and 225,000 rounds of ammunition.

Mother Jones wanted the rest of the country to know what was going on in West Virginia, so she took to the road once more and delivered speeches in eastern and midwestern cities to gain sympathy for the striking miners.

In February 1913, tragic violence brought the nation's attention to West Virginia's coal war. Some striking miners were living with their families in a tent city at Holly Grove. Company guards were stationed in a nearby settlement and the two groups frequently shot at each other. After one encounter, the mine guards boarded a train mounted with a machine gun and steamed through the tent colony spraying gunfire. They killed one miner and wounded a woman. No one was arrested.

Outraged at the lack of justice being provided for the strikers, Mother Jones took a group of thirty miners to talk to the state's governor. By the time they had boarded the train to Charleston, rumors had traveled ahead of them. Word spread that Mother Jones had thirty-five hundred miners with her and that she planned to kill the governor.

The rumors gave the state militia the excuse they had been looking for. When she reached Charleston Mother Jones was arrested and sent to a nearby town. She was charged with stealing a machine gun, blowing up a train, and conspiring to murder.

Because the strike area was under martial law, she was tried in a military court even though the civil courts were still open. Mother Jones refused to make a plea because she considered the military court illegal. There was no hearing and no trial but she was imprisoned anyway.

For several weeks she was locked in a cabin on the banks of the

IN WEST VIRGINIA.   THE DEATH SPECIAL

They Asked Bread And Were Given Bullets

The horror at Holly Grove, West Virginia, as shown in a newspaper illustration.

Kanawha River. Two guards watched her and she was not allowed to speak to anyone. While she was there the voters of West Virginia elected Henry Hatfield, a medical doctor, to become the state's new governor. Though he had the support of the mine owners, he also had sympathy for the miners and decided to visit Mother Jones.

Governor Hatfield found her "lying on a straw tick on the floor, carrying a temperature of 104, very rapid respiration, and a constant cough. She had pneumonia." The governor sent her to Charleston to recover, but as soon as she was well she was back in prison.

Mother Jones always had a knack for making friends with people who could help her. This time she won over one of her guards and persuaded him to smuggle out a letter she had written to Senator John Kern in Washington. Kern was a pro-labor Senator who had called for an investigation of the West Virginia coal strike. He read the letter on the floor of the Senate to his colleagues and reporters. Magazines and newspapers ran articles calling for Mother Jones's release, and soon she had gained so much sympathy Governor Hatfield was only too glad to free the little old lady in the black dress.

The governor also appointed a committee to listen to both the coal operators and the miners and to decide on an agreement both groups could live with. Shortly after the settlement the miners struck again and finally won an eight-hour day and the end of the mine guard system.

By the time the strike was over, Mother Jones had spent eighty-five days in jail and fifty men had been killed. But, as she later announced in a speech in Washington, "I didn't come out on a stretcher. I raised hell."

Mother Jones on the march in Colorado.

CHAPTER TWELVE

Ludlow

WHEN MOTHER JONES STEPPED OFF the train in Trinidad, Colorado, in 1913, one of the first things she saw was a skull and crossbones with her name written beneath it. The coal operators were not happy to see her back in the state.

Nothing had changed much in Colorado since she left. Miners in the southern part of the state were still working a twelve-hour day in unsafe mines, earning a pittance. They lived in company-owned hovels where unsanitary conditions caused outbreaks of typhoid fever, and they still had to buy their food with scrip at overpriced company stores.

For their part, the companies claimed the miners were ungrateful, uneducated, and unruly. The organizers from the UMWA were considered outside troublemakers who came into the area and stirred up violence. To the mine owners, Mother Jones was the worst of the lot. She was elderly and popular with the public and knew how to gain publicity for the miners.

Most city and state officials sided with the coal companies. The courts issued injunctions forbidding miners from picketing, congregating, or posting notices for meetings. Mine guards enforced the injunctions and Baldwin-Felts guards were brought in with machine guns. Some of the guns had been used in the recent strikes in West Virginia.

In September, more than ten thousand Colorado miners walked off

Mother Jones delivers a Labor Day speech to Colorado miners.

A miners' tent colony in Walsenburg, Colorado.

their jobs striking for higher wages, improved conditions, and the right to join the union. The miners in the southern part of the state were evicted from their company-owned homes, so they and their families gathered up their household goods and marched solemnly to tents pitched nearby.

Both the companies and the miners were armed and ready to fight. The company guards trained searchlights and machine guns on the tent colonies and drove their dreaded armored car, the "Death Special," through the streets to threaten the miners. Violence began, and Colorado's governor, Elias Ammons, sent the militia to the Trinidad area. At first the miners welcomed the troops. But before long they discovered that the militia favored the coal operators. In fact, many members of the militia were former Baldwin-Felts guards.

When Governor Ammons came to Trinidad to check out what was going on, Mother Jones boldly marched a group of miners' wives to his hotel. They swarmed into the lobby, banged on his door, and shouted for him to come out. But the governor stayed hidden in his room.

Her next move was to travel to Washington to encourage the federal government to investigate the Colorado strike. Back in the state again, she urged the miners to continue their fight. Then she traveled to El

Colorado state militiamen, armed with a machine gun, fix their gunsights on the Ludlow tent colony.

Mother Jones leads a procession of miners in Denver.

Paso, Texas, to urge Mexican strikebreakers to stay home rather than take the jobs of Colorado miners.

When she came back to Trinidad, the militia was waiting. They deported her, putting her on the train to Denver. From the window she called out to her supporters, "If they shoot me, I will talk from the grave."

Mother Jones rarely went shopping, but in Denver she spent five hundred dollars—all for shoes for the Trinidad miners and their families. Knowing that she would not be able to get back to Trinidad if officials saw her get on the train at the station, she slipped through the rail yard and climbed on the train from the rear. Again her friends on the railroads helped her. When the train made an unscheduled stop a few miles outside of Trinidad, Mother Jones got off and walked into town unnoticed by the officials who were watching for her.

Before long, however, they caught up with her. This time they sent her to San Rafael Hospital, where she was held a prisoner for nine weeks. She was sick, the state officials said, and resting comfortably. But the public knew better.

Mother Jones sasses back the governor of Colorado.

Mother Jones helps a miner's daughter put on her new shoes.

Miners' wives parade in Trinidad, Colorado, for Mother Jones's release from the San Rafael hospital.

When the women of Trinidad organized a public protest for her release, the state militia was sent in to keep order. General John Chase, head of the militia, hated the union and supported the mine owners. When he accidentally fell off his horse, the women laughed uproariously. Outraged, he ordered the men to ride into the crowd of women with their sabers drawn. The publicity that followed this incident did more for Mother Jones and her supporters than it did for General Chase and his soldiers.

General Chase described Mother Jones to Governor Ammons as an "eccentric figure" whose speeches were "coarse, vulgar, and profane." Her hot tongue inspired many of the murders and much of the violence committed by the miners, he told Ammons.

When she was released from the hospital, Mother Jones was back in Trinidad, but not for long. The military arrested her again and sent her to nearby Walsenburg. There they locked her in the cellar of the courthouse.

It was a "cold, horrible place," Mother Jones wrote, and she had to fight off rats with a bottle. There was no formal charge against her, yet she was held there for twenty-six days. Ever the fighter, she once again smuggled a letter out to the public. "Not even my incarceration in a damp underground dungeon will make me give up the fight in which I am engaged for the liberty and the rights of the working people," she wrote.

She headed to Washington as soon as she was released. There she spoke before a group of congressmen, telling them of the situation in Colorado. In her testimony she tended to ramble on and not answer questions directly. But she kept the congressmen entertained with her anecdotes and gave them a good idea of just how terrible the strike in Colorado had become. When she was asked if she had ever encouraged violence, she stoutly declared, "Never in the world."

John D. Rockefeller, Jr., whose family owned the Colorado Fuel and Iron Company, testified too. He spoke of the advantages given to the miners at his company and said unions were not necessary. But he did admit to the congressmen that he had not been to visit his family's company for more than ten years and did not really know the conditions. "You should come to Colorado," Mother Jones told him, to see the horrors first hand.

The horrors in southern Colorado were to become even more horrible, however. In 1914, the war between the miners and the company guards grew even more bitter. In Ludlow, a small mining community near Trinidad, one thousand people were living in two hundred tents. The miners were a diverse group, representing more than twenty different nationalities.

April twentieth was a Greek national holiday and the Greeks in the community were celebrating in the tent colony. They were singing and dancing and the mood seemed festive, despite the recent threats from the militia whose tent camp was nearby. Suddenly a bomb went off and smoke filled the air.

Mrs. Dominski, a miner's wife who was living in the Ludlow tent colony at the time, later gave this account at a hearing in New York: "I saw a man with a handkerchief in each hand come running up the road. He said, 'Get back and scatter.' Then another bomb was fired and I hurried to the pump station and went into the well."

She told of finding her two children in the well, a cavern about eighteen feet wide where about eighty people were hiding.

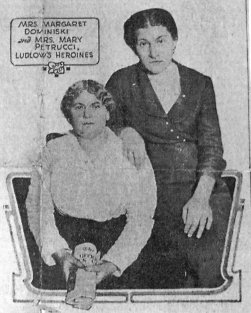
A newspaper reports the story told by two Ludlow survivors.

"I grabbed my other child and ran to a barn, after I had been warned that we'd be shot if we stayed in the well. Later my little girl started for the barn; she was shot at before she reached it. The militia also shot at my boy as he ran across."

She described how later that day she saw the militia set fire to the tents. "I saw six or eight of them burning them. Three men had torches that looked like ignited brooms and others had cans. I think there was oil in them. The train was coming so we ran along, sheltered by it, to the station. The bullets just whizzed past us. As we went one woman tried to get under a fence. A bullet passed into her hip. Another exploded right in front of a woman with a baby in her arms." Other reports told of a young boy who was shot through the head while eating dinner in his tent.

When the day of terror was over, twelve children, two women, and five men were dead. The nation was stunned and horrified by what had happened at Ludlow. The guards had become a vicious mob. For ten

The body of a miner killed by the militia during the Ludlow massacre.

Newspaper reporters protect themselves from violence with a white truce flag while viewing the ruins at Ludlow.

Funeral for the victims of Ludlow.

days following the massacre the miners retaliated by burning company buildings and destroying the mines.

Governor Ammons called on President Woodrow Wilson to send in federal troops to restore order. The miners were allowed to rebuild their tents and the companies were no longer allowed to bring in strike-breakers. Later the federal government proposed a three-year truce during which the companies would rehire the striking miners. The United Mine Workers voted to accept the proposal, but the operators refused it.

After the Ludlow massacre, Mother Jones traveled the country telling its tragic story and raising money for its victims. By December, the union voted to end the strike and the men returned to work. Miners who had been making $3.40 a day were now paid $3.00. One of the wives whose children had been killed observed, "But then there was a family to support. Now there is only himself and me."

"UNITED WE STAND" DIVIDED WE FALL

UNITED MINE WORKERS JOURNAL

ORGANIZATION   JUSTICE   EDUCATION

VOL. XXIV. No. 52   INDIANAPOLIS, IND., THURSDAY, MAY 7, 1914. $1.00 PER YEAR

Militia and Guards Burned Women and Babies, Jury Finds

Federal Troops Bring Peace in Strike Zone

Strikers Repulse Militia Mine Guards

Slaughter at Colony is Laid to Tools of Operators

Many Die in Mine Horror

THE VULTURE AND ITS PREY

A drawing in the United Mine Workers Journal lambasts John D. Rockefeller, Jr., after the Ludlow Massacre.

Mother Jones shakes hands with John D. Rockefeller, Jr. Photo from New York Tribune.

After the Ludlow Massacre Mother Jones and John D. Rockefeller, Jr., again testified in Washington about conditions in the coal fields. This time, Rockefeller invited his long-time critic to visit him in his office. He charmed her.

"What I like about young Mr. Rockefeller is that he's so approach-able," she told a newspaper reporter. "I can sit and talk to him just as I do to you. . . . I misjudged that young man sadly. I called him a high class burglar. I told him so. . . . He laughed, and I must say he took it good-naturedly. But I know him better now, and after talking with him he knows more about his father's mines in Colorado too."

Conditions in the Colorado mines did improve over the next several years, and the public became more sympathetic to labor than it had been before. But many workers still remained bitter toward the coal companies.

Some of her supporters thought Mother Jones had sold out by talk-ing with Rockefeller, but she continued her wholehearted support of the miners and the union. According to her calculations, she was in her mid-eighties in 1915. Anyone else would have used age as an excuse to slow down and retire from the front lines of the labor wars. Slowing down was not something Mother Jones did easily, however. As long as she was able she would find more battles to fight.

Mother Jones in her flower-trimmed hat meets with President Calvin Coolidge.

CHAPTER THIRTEEN

The Woman with an "Excess of Courage"

DURING THE YEARS FOLLOWING the Ludlow Massacre, Mother Jones crisscrossed the country supporting a variety of causes. One was the defense of her friend and fellow labor organizer, Tom Mooney.

Mooney, a radical and a Socialist, had been accused of planting a bomb which exploded at a parade in San Francisco in 1916. Mother Jones did not always agree with Mooney's point of view, but she thought he was innocent of planting the bomb.

When she traveled to California to speak in his defense, a San Francisco newspaper said she "stood up like one inspired, her face struck with intense emotion, her deep, resonant voice ringing with power." When Mooney was sentenced to hang, Mother Jones intervened with the governor to have his sentence reduced to life imprisonment. Years later, he was finally set free.

During the next three years, Mother Jones was in Indiana campaigning for the reelection of Senator Kern, investigating prison conditions in West Virginia, and urging the wives of New York City streetcar workers to support their husbands' strike.

In 1919 she returned to the coal fields of West Virginia to help organize Logan and Mingo counties in the southern part of the state. Though she was by now quite old, she had lost none of her fighting spirit. Years later, Monia Baumgartner, a miner's wife who lived in this area as a young woman, reminisced about traveling with Mother Jones to one of her nighttime meetings in the woods.

Mother Jones was staying with Monia's family and asked the young woman to go with her one evening. "Oh, Mrs. Jones, I can't go with you . . ." she replied. "You ain't afraid and I am."

But Mother Jones persuaded her and together they bumped their way across the rutted mountain roads. Instead of wearing her usual black dress Mother Jones wore a pair of men's coveralls, high-topped boots, and a man's hat pulled down on her head. Under the wagon seat she carried a big club to ward off attackers.

When the two reached the clearing in the woods, Mother Jones began one of her organizing harangues. She chastised the men for being cowards in the fight against the coal operators and for allowing their wives and children to live in poverty.

"Then all at once, KA-WHOOM!" Monia recalled. "A bullet went right between our heads and I'm a'telling you that liked to scare me to death. I said, 'Now listen here, old woman, I'm getting out of here.'"

Mother Jones, however, just kept on talking. "Well you can shoot again," she yelled out. "You missed me that time." Young Monia was

Mother Jones follows the flag in a parade of striking steel workers.

Mother Jones marching for the steel workers in Pennsylvania.

relieved to reach home safely and in spite of several invitations, she never went out with Mother Jones again.

It was also in 1919, when the nation's steel workers were preparing to go out on strike, that Mother Jones led a march of ten thousand men in Pennsylvania protesting the suspension of free speech. For that she was arrested. In Duquesne, the mayor firmly said she would not be allowed to speak there. Defiantly, she did so anyway, and was arrested again and fined one hundred dollars.

In Gary, Indiana, another steel-mill town, Mother Jones made one of her most inflammatory speeches. "I'll be ninety years old the first of May," she told her audience, "but by God if I have to, I'll take ninety guns and shoot . . . 'em. . . . We'll hang the bloodhounds to the telegraph poles." This was one of her most radical speeches. Perhaps she felt she had to prove that she had not mellowed with age.

After the Gary speech, the *New York Times* called Mother Jones a Bolshevik, a name that had come to represent unpatriotic, un-American agitators. Generally, the press and the public were unsympathetic to the strike. When the UMWA refused to support the steel workers by calling a sympathy strike, the steel strike failed. Mother Jones never forgave John L. Lewis, who was then the president of the coal union.

The one luxury Mother Jones allowed herself during her lifetime was a trip to Mexico City in 1921 to speak at an international labor meeting. General Antonio Villareal, one of the Mexican revolutionaries she had supported, wrote to invite her saying, "We have a house ready for you and a prettier place cannot be imagined. Also servants and an automobile."

This was a life Mother Jones was not accustomed to. She was treated like royalty and loved it. She rode in a special train and Mexican workers showered her with flowers along the way. For the first time in her life, she had servants and a chauffeur to drive her through the streets of Mexico City.

By summer of that year she was back in West Virginia lending support to the striking miners there. Coal companies had hired deputies to help keep union organizers out of their state and several union men were arrested. The miners organized a huge march to demand the men be set free. The state's governor feared the march would get out of hand. He went so far as to ask the federal government to help with troops.

Mother Jones, uncharacteristically, urged caution on the part of "her boys." At a rally of the miners she waved a telegram in the air, telling the men it was from President Warren G. Harding and that it promised an investigation of their grievances and an end to the mine guard system. The telegram turned out to be a fake, and Mother Jones lost face with some of her former supporters.

Mother Jones was now suffering from rheumatism and was exhausted from her travels to Mexico and West Virginia. In 1922 she went to Washington, D.C., to stay with her old friends Terrance and Emma Powderly. Many of her supporters thought she was near death. But she rallied and soon was off to Illinois and Indiana. In Fort Wayne she lent encouragement to some striking shopmen, and wrote to a

No work tomorrow.

West Virginia miners evicted from their homes in 1924.

Mother Jones and Terrance Powderly.

friend, "I feel if I am able to crawl I owe them a duty to give them a word of encouragement."

Her next project was to write her autobiography. She chose to work in Chicago, the city where she had begun her life as a labor organizer. Between the hours of working on her book, she found time to support the dressmakers who were out on strike. It was her last appearance on the front lines of a labor strike.

Writing a book did not suit Mother Jones. She was used to tramping the gullies of West Virginia and living in tents, and she complained in letters to friends of being inactive. She also scolded her friend Terrance Powderly for his fear of old age. "Don't be looking forward to the day you go away . . . look forward to the great grand work you have done in the past and the work there is to do in the future."

But even Mother Jones was less and less able to think of the future.

In 1929, she moved in with a family in Silver Spring, Maryland, where she spent most of her time in bed.

On May 1, 1930, she celebrated her one hundredth birthday. There was always some confusion about how old Mother Jones *really* was, for she often gave conflicting information about her age. Whatever the exact truth was, she had lived a very long and full life. Friends from all over came to visit and she received a cake with one hundred candles on it.

One of many newspaper accounts of Mother Jones's one hundredth birthday.

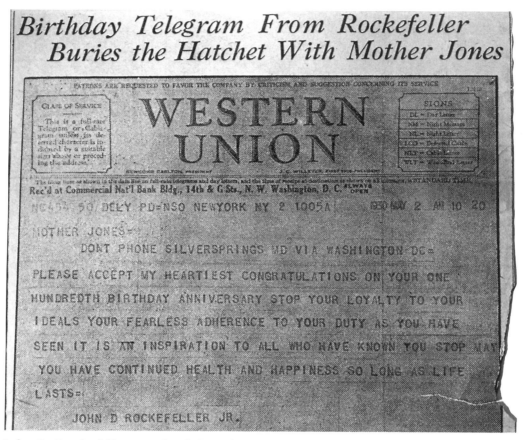

Birthday Telegram From Rockefeller Buries the Hatchet With Mother Jones

WESTERN UNION

John D. Rockefeller, Jr.'s birthday telegram to Mother Jones.

The newspapers ran stories and photos of the event, and John D. Rockefeller, Jr., sent her a congratulatory telegram. "He's a damn good sport," she told a newspaper reporter. "I've licked him many times but now we've made peace."

A few months later, Rockefeller's father celebrated his ninety-first birthday and she sent a birthday greeting. But she told a friend, "I wouldn't trade what I've done for what he's done."

As the months passed, Mother Jones, now almost blind, grew weaker and spent her days lying in a four-poster bed. By late fall it was clear that she was near death. Reporters, bundled up against the November cold, camped out in cars outside the Silver Spring house.

Occasionally she would rally enough to talk about her earlier life.

Quiet, Not Cake, Features John D.'s 91st Birthday

Photograph by A. P

OHN D. ROCKEFELLER, Who Peacefully Celebrated His Birthday o
His Pocantico Hills Estate Yesterday

Mother Jones and Boy Scouts Among Those Sendin;
Greetings; Family Dinner Party Ends Peaceful Day

Mother Jones smooths things over with the senior Rockefeller.

She remembered hearing Abraham Lincoln speak out against slavery. Men like Lincoln are "hard to find these days," she said.

Indeed, men like Lincoln are hard to find in any time. So too are women like Mother Jones. When she died on November 30, 1930, newspapers all over the country featured photos and stories on their front pages honoring the Chicago seamstress. Union presidents, miners, and friends crowded the Washington church for her requiem mass. Eight pallbearers, each one from a different trade union, carried her casket. At the back of the church dozens of unemployed men stood, paying tribute.

The Mother Jones monument at the union miners' cemetery in Mount Olive.

Mourners line up to view Mother Jones's body.

After the mass in Washington, her casket was put on a Baltimore and Ohio train bound for Saint Louis. From Saint Louis, it was taken to Mount Olive, a tiny town in the heart of the southern Illinois coal fields. On the outskirts of town lies a cemetery dedicated to union miners where she had asked to be buried.

Her body lay in state in the Odd Fellows hall in Mount Olive for two

The funeral parade in Mount Olive, Illinois.

days. The town had never seen such crowds. Thousands of miners thronged the hall to say farewell to their champion.

A formal funeral was held at Mount Olive's Roman Catholic Church of the Ascension on December 7. Newspaper reporters, movie cameras, cars, and more than ten thousand spectators showed up for the service. The church could hold only three hundred and the crowds thronged the streets.

In his eulogy, the priest spoke of Mother Jones's "burning conviction that oppression must end." He spoke of her "eloquent and flaming tongue that won men to her cause" and her "consuming love for the

The overflow crowd at Mother Jones's funeral in Mount Olive.

poor." Her faults, he said, were the "excess of her courage" and the "love in her mother's heart."

In the years following her death, admirers honored Mother Jones's memory with festivals, plays, and books. A magazine was named for her and a monument was erected at her gravesite.

The United States Department of Labor installed a special Mother Jones display in the lobby of its Washington, D.C., headquarters. There visitors can see a videotape of Mother Jones and hear her speaking in her still-noticeable Irish brogue. Her old pocketbook is there and so is one of her hats.

A poster commemorating Mother Jones captures her fighting spirit.

Many songs and poems were written in her honor. One, in particular, sums up the miners' affection and admiration for their heroine:

> *Do they think an injunction will gag Mother Jones?*
> *It will certainly fail—*
> *Though they've put her in jail*
> *Or keep her surrounded by prison wall stones,*
> *There are thousands to talk for old Mother Jones.*
>
> *For the words and the works of old Mother Jones*
> *For downtrodden men*
> *Will be eulogized when*
> *The earth has enshrouded the weary old bones*
> *And a monument built for old Mother Jones.*
>
> *Then the wonderful spirit of old Mother Jones*
> *May march up and down*
> *Like the soul of John Brown.*
> *Till justice shall vanquish our burdens and groans,*
> *And oppression is buried like old Mother Jones.*

106

Acknowledgments and Photo Credits

MANY PEOPLE GAVE GENEROUSLY of their time and knowledge during my research for this book. I particularly thank Lois McLean, whom many regard as the foremost authority on Mother Jones. I am also indebted to Roger Bruns, the National Archives; Carrie Bruns, Smithsonian Books; Richard Conn, Friends of the Department of Labor; Thelma Blount, the United Mine Workers of America; Helen Harvey, Northwestern Medical Library; Judson McClury, Department of Labor; Leslie Orear, the Illinois Labor History Society; Thomas Zito, Catholic University Archives; and the staffs of the Library of Congress Print and Photo Division, The Chicago Historical Society, and the Newberry Library.

Portions of *The Autobiography of Mother Jones* appear on pages: 2, 3, 5, 8, 10, 14, 17, 22, 25, 27, 28, 34, 36, 41, 42, 48, 50, 53, 54, 55, 59, 63, 66, 72, 84, 85.

Excerpts from "I'll Teach You Not to Be Afraid" by Lois McLean, published in *Goldenseal*, January–March, 1980, appear on page 94.

The poem, "Mother Jones," by Oscar Langford, reprinted on page 106, was found in manuscript form in the Department of Archives and Manuscripts, The Catholic University of America, Washington, D.C.

Photographs and other illustrations were provided courtesy of:
Library of Congress: pages 6, 11, 13, 14, 15, 18, 19, 21, 22, 23, 24, 26, 29, 30, 32, 35, 38, 39, 40, 42, 44, 52, 54, 55, 56 (bottom), 57, 60, 87, 92, 106

U.S. Department of Labor: pages 56 (top), 76

United Mine Workers of America: pages 46, 47, 49, 50, 51, 62, 67 (top), 83 (top), 84, 89, 97

Illinois Labor History Society: pages 80, 98, 102, 103, 104, 105

The Newberry Library: pages 64, 74, 78, 82, 83 (bottom), 88, 94, 95

Colorado Historical Society: pages 65, 67 (bottom), 81

The Catholic University of America: pages 86, 90, 99, 100, 101

West Virginia and Regional History Collection: pages 70, 73

Notes

How Old Was Mother Jones?

NO ONE SEEMS TO KNOW exactly how old Mother Jones was. Her own accounts of her birthdate ranged from 1830 to 1844. Perhaps she liked people to believe she was older than she really was, since it enhanced the drama of her escapades in the labor movement. Lois McLean, a prominent Mother Jones scholar from Beckley, West Virginia, has found parish records in Ireland that indicate she was probably born in 1837.

Mother Jones and the Law

Throughout her career Mother Jones was always embroiled with the intricacies of the United States legal and judicial system. She often knowingly violated injunctions, or legal court orders, to pursue a cause she thought was just. Like protesters of later years, she was willing to pay the consequences and go to jail, since she knew that her imprisonment would bring attention to her cause.

When she was arrested without formal charges in Trinidad, Colorado, in 1913 she gained her freedom through a writ of *habeas corpus*, a constitutionally guaranteed right that allows prisoners to be released unless the government can produce concrete evidence against them.

During the 1919 steel strike, she and fellow labor leaders deliberately violated ordinances or spoke without the necessary permits in order to bring attention to what they considered a violation of the right to freedom of speech.

One of the purposes of her march of the mill children in 1903 was to force the federal government to pass a law prohibiting the hiring of children to work in factories. Congress did not pass such a law until 1916. Even then, it was soon declared unconstitutional. In 1918 Congress passed a similar law, but it too was struck down. It was not until 1938 that child labor was made illegal when the Supreme Court ruled in favor of the Fair Labor Standards Act.

Why Mother Jones Is Buried in Mount Olive

Mother Jones is buried in a cemetery in the quiet community of Mount Olive, Illinois. She lies alongside seven coal miners who were killed in a 1898 labor uprising in the nearby town of Virden. In a dispute over wages, southern Illinois coal operators tried to bring in scabs to take the jobs of striking coal miners. When the miners rebelled, forty miners were wounded and seven were killed. The miners' families were not allowed to bury the men in the local cemetery, so the union bought land in Mount Olive and created its own cemetery there. Mother Jones regarded those killed at Virden as great heroes and an inspiration to the labor movement. It was her wish that she rest with them.

More About Mother Jones

THOSE WANTING TO KNOW MORE about Mother Jones should read *The Autobiography of Mother Jones* (The Charles H. Kerr Publishing Company, Chicago, 1990). It was written late in her life when her memory was beginning to fade and it contains several inaccuracies and exaggerations. But it also embodies her spirited opinions and there are excellent notes at the end by labor historian Fred Thompson which help sort out fact from fiction.

To gain an understanding of her colorful speaking style, consult *The Speeches and Writings of Mother Jones*, edited by Edward M. Steel (The University of Pittsburgh Press, Pittsburgh, Pennsylvania, 1988), which offers a well-documented collection of her speeches from 1901 through 1922. Steel has also edited *The Correspondence of Mother Jones* (The University of Pittsburgh Press, Pittsburgh, Pennsylvania, 1985).

Dale Fetherling's *Mother Jones: The Miners' Angel, A Portrait* (Southern Illinois University Press, Carbondale, Illinois, 1974) is a thorough and highly readable account of Mother Jones's life and the labor events that surrounded it.

Two masters' theses were particularly helpful in researching this book: Helen Collier Camp's "Mother Jones and the Children's

Crusade" (Columbia University, 1970) and Judith Elaine Mikeal's "Mother Mary Jones: The Labor Movement's Impious Joan of Arc" (University of North Carolina, 1965).

The archives at Catholic University of America in Washington, D.C., include the papers of Mother Jones, and The Charles H. Kerr Company, the Chicago-based publisher of her autobiography, maintains a collection of Mother Jones memorabilia as does Chicago's Newberry Library.

Index

Page numbers in *italics* refer to illustrations.

About the Author

BETSY HARVEY KRAFT wanted to be an author from the time she could hold a pencil, but took a long detour as an editor of children's books, an association executive, and an educator before fulfilling her childhood ambition. She knew of Mother Jones for years before she found a collection of her speeches and was inspired to share her extraordinary life with young adult readers. She particularly enjoyed unearthing photographs that portrayed the turbulent times on the front lines of the labor conflicts, and was moved by the monument to Mother Jones that stands in the quiet miners' cemetery in southern Illinois.

Ms. Kraft lives in Washington, D.C. *Mother Jones: One Woman's Fight for Labor* is her fourth book for young readers and her first biography.